# DO IT YOURSELF

# Watching Wildlife

## *Animal Habitats*

**Carol Ballard**

Heinemann Library
Chicago, Illinois

Customer Service 888-454-2279
Visit our website at www.heinemannraintree.com

Editorial: Louise Galpine and Catherine Veitch
Design: Richard Parker and Tinstar Design Ltd
Illustrations: ODI
Picture Research: Mica Brancic and Elaine Willis
Production: Victoria Fitzgerald

Originated by Chroma Graphics (Overseas) Pte. Ltd
Printed and bound in China by Leo Paper Group

12 11 10 09 08
10 9 8 7 6 5 4 3 2 1

**Library of Congress Cataloging-in-Publication Data**
Ballard, Carol.
Watching wildlife : animal habitats / Carol Ballard.
   p. cm. -- (Do it yourself science)
Includes bibliographical references and index.
ISBN 978-1-4329-1087-7 (hc) -- ISBN 978-1-4329-1103-4 (pb)  1. Wildlife watching--Juvenile literature. 2. Habitat
(Ecology)--Juvenile literature.  I. Title. II. Title: Animal habitats.
QL60.B355 2008
591.7--dc22
                            2007050503

**Acknowledgments**
The publishers would like to thank the following for permission to reproduce photographs: ©Alamy pp. **4** (James Clarke
Images), **7** (Arco Images), **26-27** (Ashley Cooper); ©Corbis pp. **9** (Papillo/Ken Wilson), **11** (Anthony Redpath), **14** (Robert
Estall), **15** (Wolfgang Kaehler), **19** (zefa/Alexander Benz), **20** (Andy Rouse), **31** (Buddy Mays), **35** (zefa/Herbert Kehrer),
**36** (Kevin Schafer), **37** (Ecoscene/Wayne Lawler), **41** (zefa/Herbert Spichtinger), **43** (Michael & Patricia Fogden); ©Getty
Images pp. **4** (Jeff Foott), **13** (National Geographic/Joel Sartore), **17** (Minden Pictures/Michael Durham), **21** (Catherine
Ledner), **25** (Geoff Dann), **29** (The Image Bank/Derek P. Redfearn), **32** (Renaud Visage), **33** (Steve & Ann Toon), **34** (Harald
Sund), **39** (Stone/Ian Murphy), **42** (Kevin Schafer); ©Photolibrary p. **6** (Digital Vision/GK Hart/Vikki Hart).

Cover photograph of a polar bear, reproduced with permission of Photolibrary/Alaskastock/Steven Kazlowski.

Every effort has been made to contact copyright holders of any material reproduced in this book.
Any omissions will be rectified in subsequent printings if notice is given to the publishers.

The publishers would like to thank Nick Lapthorn for his help in the preparation of this book.

# Contents

**Warning:** Always wash your hands after touching wild animals or plants.

Any words appearing in the text in bold, **like this**, are explained in the glossary.

# Wildlife All Around Us

Our planet is home to many millions of different living things! There is wildlife all around us, whether we are at home, in school, in a park, or out in the country. There are even living things in the middle of cities. Plants grow in places where you cannot see any soil for them. Lichens can grow on stones, and tufts of grass can spring up just about anywhere. Living creatures such as flies, beetles, and birds are always nearby, even if we do not notice them.

This coyote lives in a natural, dry desert habitat in Utah.

## In the garden

Gardens and other open spaces are home to many types of wildlife. Plants such as trees can be huge, while others, such as **mosses**, are tiny. Some creatures live in the soil, some live on the ground, some live on plants, and some even live on other creatures.

## What is a habitat?

The place where a plant or creature lives is called its **habitat**. Land that has not been changed by people provides a natural habitat. In places where people have changed the land, habitats are made by humans. Sometimes these changes are good for the wildlife. Making a new garden pond creates a perfect habitat for water plants, fish, newts, and dragonflies. Sometimes changes are bad for wildlife. Building new roads, houses, and factories can destroy precious natural habitats.

**Warning**: Do not touch fungi. Some are poisonous.

Look at fungi carefully. They are amazing. Tiny **spores** fall from the underside of the caps to grow into new fungi.

## Stay safe!

Wherever you go and whatever you do, it is important to do all you can to stay safe. Make sure you remember to do the following:

- Check with an adult to make sure that what you want to do is safe.
- Always tell an adult where you are going, whom you are going with, and what time you expect to be back.
- Wear the right kind of clothing for the place you are visiting.
- Obey all instructions, warning signs, and safety signs.
- Be careful—do not take any unnecessary risks!

# Being a Nature Detective

Living things come in all sorts of shapes, sizes, and colors. There are tall trees, tiny creepy crawlies, dull gray mice, and parrots with brightly colored feathers. There are slimy blobs of jellyfish, and butterflies with a delicate structure. There seems to be no end to the variety of wildlife on our planet.

A variety of fish are kept in this aquarium. Can you identify some different characteristics of these fish?

## What are characteristics?

If you go into a classroom, you will probably see tables, chairs, books, and computers. These are the things that tell you it is a classroom rather than another type of room, such as a gym. Things like this are called the **characteristics** of a classroom. Living things have characteristics, too. The characteristics of a goldfish include **scales**, **fins**, a tail, and an orangey-gold color. The characteristics of a tortoise include a strong shell, four legs, and a long neck that can be tucked under the shell.

## Natural variations

Some plants, such as sunflowers, have large, bright flowers, while others, such as oak trees, have tiny, dull flowers. Sharks can swim, while eagles can fly. Cheetahs can run fast, while tortoises move slowly. Tigers have striking patterns on their bodies, while polar bears are a plain color all over. Sheep eat plants, while wolves eat other animals. All of these characteristics tell us something about each plant and creature.

Peregrine falcons are the fastest birds in the world. They can dive at speeds of nearly 180 mph (288 kmh)!

This chart shows some amazing wildlife facts:

| Record-breaker | Name |
| --- | --- |
| Biggest animal in the world | Blue whale: More than 65 feet (20 m) long and weighing more than 100 tons (100,000 kg) |
| Biggest land animal | African elephant: Up to 13 feet (4 m) high, 30 feet (9 m) long (from trunk to tail), and weighing up to 8.5 tons (8,000 kg) |
| Fastest runner | Cheetah: Runs at up to 60 mph (100 kmh) when hunting |
| Fastest flier | Peregrine falcon: Dives at nearly 180 mph (288 kmh) |
| Longest life | Turtle and tortoise: Can live for more than 200 years |
| Shortest life | Adult mayfly: Lives for just a few hours |
| Biggest egg | Ostrich: Eggs can weigh 3 to 4 pounds (1.7 kg) |

## Steps to follow

**1** First, ask an adult if you can collect some soil from outside. Scoop a few handfuls into a plastic tray. Be careful not to disturb any plants growing nearby.

**2** Use a small plastic spoon to spread the soil out until there is just a thin layer on the tray. Look carefully. Can you see any tiny creatures moving around in the soil?

**3** Observe the creatures carefully and try to describe some of them. Ask yourself questions such as: Does it have a shell? How many legs does it have? Can I see its eyes? Try to draw a simple sketch of some of the creatures. You might find a **magnifying glass** useful.

**4** When you have finished looking at your soil sample, take it back to where it came from. Tip the soil back on to the garden—but be careful and try not to harm any of the living creatures!

**Warning**: Always wash your hands thoroughly after touching soil!

## Grouping living things

If you look at a group of your friends, you could sort them into groups in several ways. For example, you could sort them into those who wear glasses and those who do not wear glasses. You could sort them into those with curly hair and those with straight hair. If you do this, you are using their characteristics to sort them into groups.

It is important to look carefully if you want to see all the details of a creature like this beetle.

When scientists want to sort living things into groups, they look at their characteristics and find ways in which they are alike (similarities) and ways in which they are different (differences).

Look at your sketches of the soil creatures. Can you find some similarities and differences among them? One way of sorting them might be into a group with long bodies and a group with bodies that are not long. Can you think of any other ways of sorting them?

## Pressing leaves

For this activity you will need:

* Two heavy books
* Newspaper
* Paper towels
* A plastic bag
* Leaves

**1** Go outside and try to find as many different types of leaves lying on the ground as you can. Carefully put each leaf in a plastic bag.

**2** Put a large book on a table. Fold a sheet of newspaper to about the same size as the book. Open the book at the back, lay the newspaper on top of the open page, and then lay a sheet of paper towel on top of the newspaper. Take a single leaf and place it on the paper towel. Cover it with another piece of paper towel and then another sheet of folded newspaper. Turn over some pages. Now repeat this for each of your leaves. Put your book where it will be undisturbed for about a month. Put another heavy book on top if it.

**3** After a month, you can carefully remove the leaves from the book. Use sticky tape to fasten your leaves into a scrapbook. Try to discover the name of your leaves and write them in your scrapbook, too.

# Sorting plants into groups

Scientists look at the similarities and differences among plants. This helps them to sort the plants into groups. Some plants are very simple, but others are quite complicated. There are five main plant groups:

- **Algae** are the simplest plants. Seaweeds are algae. They have no roots or leaves.
- **Mosses** are simple plants, too. They have leaves, but no true roots. You can see mosses growing on old stones and in damp, shady places.
- **Ferns** are more complicated than mosses. They have roots and long, spiky leaves called **fronds**. New ferns grow from **spores** on the backs of the fronds.
- **Conifers** are pine trees. They have roots and leaves, and new trees grow from **seeds** that are made inside pinecones.
- **Flowering plants** are the most complicated group of all. They have roots, leaves, and flowers. New plants grow from seeds that are made by the flowers.

Compare the leaves shown here. What similarities and differences can you see?

## Steps to follow

**1** Choose one of the pictures below. Then, look at the first question at the bottom of the page: Does it have a long tail? Decide whether it has a long tail or not. If it does, follow the "Yes" arrow. If it does not, follow the "No" arrow.

**Key**

**2** Look at the next question you come to. If it is true for your creature, follow the "Yes" arrow. If it is not true for your creature, follow the "No" arrow. Stop here if this leads to the name of the creature.

**3** If you have not found the name yet, look at the next question you come to. If it is true for your creature, follow the "Yes" arrow. If it is not true for your creature, follow the "No" arrow. This should lead to the name of the creature.

Can you find the names of each of the creatures in the pictures?

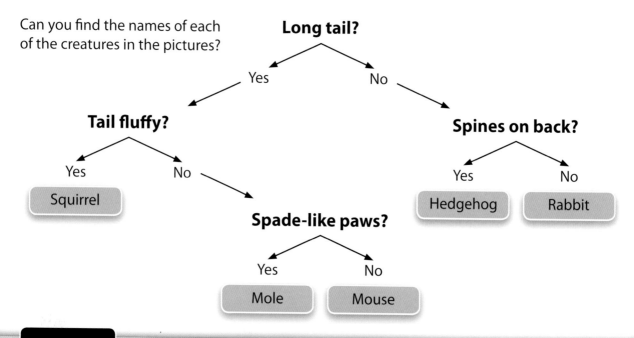

## Sorting animals into groups

Scientists organize animals into groups just as they do plants. They look at their similarities and differences. One of the characteristics they look at is whether or not the creature has a backbone. If it does, it belongs in the **vertebrate** group. If it does not, it belongs in the **invertebrate** group.

Then they look at other similarities and differences among them. Animals with backbones are sorted into five smaller groups. You can see them in this chart:

This peacock is really showing off its wonderful feathers! Do you know which group it belongs in?

| Group | Characteristics | Group includes |
|---|---|---|
| Fish | • Have scales and fins<br>• Breathe with **gills**<br>• Live in water | Salmon<br>Sticklebacks<br>Sharks |
| **Amphibians** | • Have smooth, wet skin<br>• Breathe with gills or lungs<br>• Lay eggs in water | Frogs<br>Toads<br>Newts |
| **Reptiles** | • Have dry scales<br>• Breathe with lungs<br>• Live in water or on land<br>• Lay soft-shelled eggs on land | Snakes<br>Crocodiles<br>Lizards<br>Turtles |
| Birds | • Have feathers, wings, and beaks<br>• Breathe with lungs<br>• Lay hard-shelled eggs<br>• Live on land<br>• Can control their body temperature | Eagles<br>Swans<br>Peacocks<br>Robins |
| **Mammals** | • Have hair or fur<br>• Babies develop inside mother<br>• Babies feed on mother's milk<br>• Can control their body temperature | Dolphins<br>Mice<br>Elephants<br>Humans |

# A Place to Live

Why don't elephants live in the sea or fish live in forests? Why do cacti grow in sandy deserts and polar bears live in the Arctic? It is because different **habitats** suit different living things.

Some habitats, such as oceans, forests, and deserts, are so different from each other that the plants and animals that live in one cannot survive in the other.

Other habitats may be quite similar, with only small differences. If you look in a park or garden, you might find bright, sunny spaces and dark, shady spaces. Some spaces are dry, while others are damp. Some spaces are open, while others are hidden. Differences such as these make a particular space a good habitat for some living things, but a poor habitat for others.

Look around you— habitats that are home to plants and animals can be found everywhere!

## What does a habitat provide?

A habitat has to provide everything that lives in it with three main things:

- Food and water: Plants need sunlight and water to make their own food, but animals also need plants or other animals to eat.

- Safety: Plants cannot grow well if they are being eaten or trampled all the time. Animals cannot survive if they are being hunted or if there are other dangers around them.

- Somewhere to raise their young: Plant **seeds** need the right conditions to grow into new plants. Eggs need to be able to hatch, and baby animals need to be able to grow safely into adults.

## Different needs

Different animals eat different foods. They need different conditions for safety and for bringing up their young. This means that they must live in different places. A habitat that suits one type of animal may be completely unsuitable for another type of animal.

A crocodile's ideal habitat has dry land with water nearby.

## Pond dipping

For this activity you will need:

* A plastic scoop
* A jar or clear plastic tray
* A magnifying glass

**1** Ask an adult to go with you to a safe, local pond. Use a plastic scoop to put some pond water into a jar or clear plastic tray. Be careful not to scoop up mud from the bottom of the pond, because this makes it difficult to see anything.

**2** Observe your pond water carefully. Can you see any pond creatures? A **magnifying glass** will help you to see very tiny things. Do the creatures have legs, shells, **antennae**, and tails? Look at how each creature moves. Do they swim, skip, jump, or slide?

**3** When you have finished looking, put your pond water back into the pond. Lower the jar or tray into the pond and slowly turn it upside down. This lets the water gently flow out into the pond and saves any of the living creatures from being hurt.

**Warning**: Always wash your hands after you have been pond dipping!

## What lives in a pond?

Ponds are home to a huge number of living things. The soil is damp and boggy around the edges of ponds. Plants such as irises, reeds, and rushes grow well here. Pondweed floats on the water. Water lilies have very long stalks, so their roots are in the mud at the bottom of the pond. Their flowers and leaves float on the surface of the water.

All sorts of **invertebrates** live in the mud and in the water. Other creatures, such as newts and fish, live in the water, too. Frogs and toads are often found around ponds. Birds such as ducks nest close to ponds and feed on weeds or fish.

Dragonflies are one of the fastest flying insects. They can also hover and fly backward!

## Steps to follow

### Bark rubbing

For this activity you will need:

* Plain white paper
* A wax crayon
* Some trees

**1** Ask an adult to go with you to a safe, local wood. Look at different trees and feel the bark of the trunks. Can you see and feel how different they can be from each other?

**2** When you have found a tree with interesting bark, hold a sheet of white paper against the trunk. Rub a wax crayon carefully back and forth across the paper. (Do not rub too hard or your paper might tear.) As you rub, a dark and light pattern will appear, showing the bumps and dips of the bark.

**3** Why not make rubbings from several different types of tree? You could put them together to make an interesting wall display. You could also press a leaf from each tree (explained on page 10) and display it with each bark rubbing.

## Woodland animals

There are so many different plants and animals living in a wood that it is almost impossible to count them all! Invertebrates live in the soil around tree roots, in the piles of dead leaves on the ground, on the tree bark, and on the leaves. Some animals, such as squirrels, make their nests in tree trunks, while many birds nest among the branches.

Different woodland creatures are active at different times of day. Some, such as birds and butterflies, are active during the day. Others, such as badgers and wood mice, are **nocturnal**, which means they sleep during the day and are active at night.

Have you ever touched rough, craggy bark like this?

## Woodland plants

In addition to the trees, there are many other plants in a woodland. In spring, before the leaves grow, many bulbs and other small plants flower in the sunlight. Later, as the leaves make the woodland floor shady, **ferns** and other shade-loving plants grow. **Mosses** grow on old wood, and ivy climbs tree trunks.

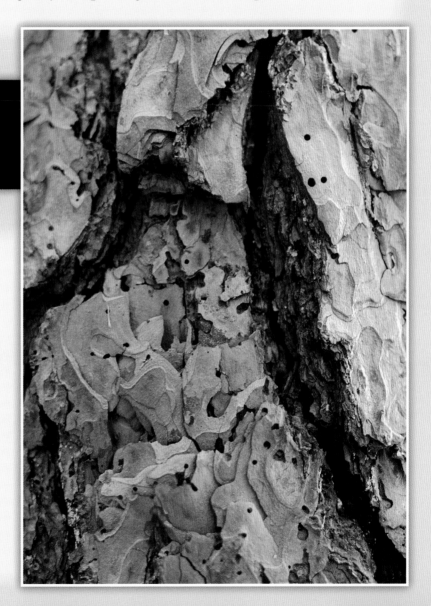

## Life by the sea

Seashores can be sandy, rocky, or pebbly. They can have steep cliffs, lumpy sand dunes, or just run out from flat land. The one thing they all have in common is that they are next to the salty water of the sea. The water moves up and down the shore twice a day in the motion that we call **tides**.

## Wet or dry?

Some things live high on the seashore and only get wet sometimes. Anything that lives around the middle of the shore has to survive being under water for part of the day and then dry for part of the day. Further down the shore, living things are under water for almost the entire day. These differences mean that different plants and creatures live in different parts of the seashore.

## Rocks and pools

Rocky surfaces are often covered in seaweed. Animals such as barnacles and limpets cling to the rocks, too.

Pools of water can be found among the rocks even when the tide goes out. These pools are perfect habitats for seaweed and small seawater creatures. If you look carefully in a rock pool, you may find sea anemones, shrimps, and tiny fish.

Turtles spend most of their lives in the sea, but they come ashore to lay their eggs.

## Sandy burrows

Some creatures such as lugworms bury themselves deep in the sand. As they burrow, they eat the sand, and their bodies use all the nutrients it contains. The waste sand then leaves their bodies and is left on the seashore as coils called worm casts.

Look on damp sand or in shallow water if you want to find a starfish.

### Static sea

The Mediterranean Sea in southern Europe does not have any big tides. The water just stays at the same level all day.

## Crabs

Crabs can be found almost anywhere on a seashore. During low tide, crabs usually hide and rest. They are most active when they are under water, especially at night.

## Seashore birds

Seabirds such as gulls are common around a seashore. Many catch fish from the sea. Some search rock pools for fish and shellfish. Some dig in the sand to unearth lugworms and other burrowing creatures.

# What Lives Where?

## Steps to follow

### Where do centipedes like to live?

For this activity you will need:

* A plastic tub
* A plastic spoon
* A plastic tray
* Paper towels
* Two pieces of cardboard
* Six or eight small stones

**1** Find a loose stone or flowerpot (not too big or heavy) outside. Ask an adult's permission to move it. Lift it up and use the spoon to gently scoop up any centipedes that are underneath it. Place them into a plastic tub.

**2** Put a sheet of paper towel on the bottom of a tray. In two corners, add a small wad of damp (not wet!) paper towel. In the other two corners, add a small wad of dry paper towel. Cover one dry and one damp corner with a piece of cardboard supported on small stones. This will make each corner different:

a) dry and light

b) damp and light

c) dry and dark

d) damp and dark

**3** Gently transfer your centipedes to the center of the tray. Leave them for 30 minutes. If they are still in the middle of the tray, leave them for longer. If they are not there, lift the cardboard from each corner. Whichever corner the centipedes are in will be the one with the conditions they like best.

**4** When you have finished, take your centipedes outside and carefully put them back where you found them.

## Adaptations

Centipedes usually live in dark, damp places. Some living things have special **characteristics** that mean they are very well suited to a particular **habitat** but not to another. A polar bear's thick fur helps it to survive the Arctic cold, but it would quickly get much too hot in a sandy desert. Fish have **gills** so they can breathe in water, but they cannot breathe on dry land. A special characteristic like this, that helps a plant or creature survive in its habitat, is called an **adaptation**. We say the plant or animal is adapted to its habitat.

## Not just grass!

For this activity you will need:

* A grassy area
* A hula hoop
* Paper and a pencil

**1** Look for a light, airy place where grass grows. The middle of a lawn would be ideal. Put the hula hoop on the grass to make a circle.

**2** On a piece of paper, make a chart with one column to list each different type of plant. Another column should have space for you to make tally marks.

**3** Look carefully at the plants inside your circle. Start with one type and write its name or draw its leaf or flower shape in the first column. Then make a tally mark for each plant of that type you find in your circle. Repeat for each different type of plant in your circle.

How many different types of plant did you find? Which was the most common?

Do the same again in a patch of grass that is shady for most of the day. Are the plants and numbers similar or different?

## Plant adaptations

Different plants are adapted to different habitats. Plants need light, water, and soil to grow well. In habitats where one of these is very limited, plants have to find special ways of surviving. Plants lose water through their leaves into the air around them. The larger the leaves, the more water they lose. Many plants that live in hot, dry habitats have tiny leaves, so they lose less water. Some even have special ways of collecting and storing any rain that falls. In very dark habitats, plants have special chemicals so that they can make as much food as possible out of the small amount of light that reaches them.

## Habitat differences

Small differences between habitats will also affect which plants grow well in them. Some plants grow better in bright sunlight, while others grow better in shade. Some prefer quite dry soil, while others do better in damp, boggy soil. This explains why a patch of grass under a tree may have a different mix of plants than a patch of grass in the middle of a sunny lawn.

Take a close look at the grass outside— you will discover that it is not just grass!

## Hiding in a country field

Wild fields in the country are interesting habitats to explore. There are lots of different plants and animals living there.

This field is alive! The plants in it are home to all sorts of animals, birds, and invertebrates.

### Field plants

Most wild fields contain many different types of plant. There might be woody plants, such as hawthorn, or climbing plants, such as clematis. Blackberries and elderberries are also found in many fields, as are a variety of colorful wildflowers. Many smaller plants, such as wild grasses, grow at the foot of these areas.

## Field animals

Wild fields provide food for many creatures. **Invertebrates** such as caterpillars, **aphids**, slugs, and snails feed on the plant leaves. Other invertebrates such as beetles and worms feed on the dead leaves at the foot of the field. Some birds such as sparrows also move among the dead leaves looking for insects to eat, while birds such as finches come to eat plant **seeds**. Other birds and small animals such as mice come to eat the berries when they ripen in the fall. Birds of **prey** such as kestrels visit the field to hunt for the small creatures that live in it.

## Country homes

The wild country field provides a habitat in which many creatures can make their homes. Robins and other birds build nests among the branches. Beetles and worms live among the dead leaves on the ground. Spiders spin their webs between the branches of the plants.

## Natural balance

Even small changes can alter the natural balance of living things within a habitat. For example, spraying weedkiller around the bottom of a wild field would kill some of the smaller plants. There would be no grass seeds for the mice. Cutting back the wild plants in spring would help to control its growth—but it could destroy birds' nests. There is a natural balance within every habitat that we should be careful not to upset. If we upset the natural balance of a habitat, it could change forever.

# Food and Feeding

## Steps to follow

**Which leaves do snails like best?**

For this activity you will need:

* Four different types of leaf
* A plastic tub
* A plastic tray
* Snails

**1** First collect four different types of leaf, such as lettuce, carrot, beech, and onion. Then carefully collect five or six snails from an outdoor area and put them in a plastic tub.

**2** Sort your leaves and put each type into a different corner of a tray. Then transfer your snails from the tub to the middle of the tray. Leave them for 30 minutes. If they have not moved, leave them a little longer.

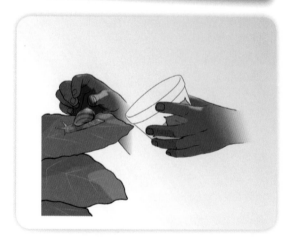

**3** Which corner have your snails moved to? You will probably find that they are all in the corner with the juiciest leaves, such as lettuce. They will have moved to the corner that has the leaves they like best.

**Warning**: Always wash your hands after touching snails. Return the snails to where you found them.

## Why do we need food?

What have you eaten today? Like every other living thing, you need food to stay alive! Food gives living things the energy they need to carry out essential processes such as pumping blood and breathing. Living things also use energy from their food for being active—for running, leaping, shouting, and flying. Food also contains the chemicals needed for growing and repairing damage.

## Plants and food

Plants also need food, but they do not eat anything. Instead they make their own food. Their leaves trap energy from sunlight and use it to make sugars and starches. The plants store these and use them when they need them. Because they produce their own food in this way, plants are called **producers**.

## Plant eaters

Animals and other creatures cannot make their own food. Instead they need to eat other living things. Different creatures eat different things. Creatures that only eat plants are called **herbivores**. Snails eat leaves, so they are herbivores.

## Meat eaters

Creatures that eat other creatures are called **carnivores**. Foxes eat chickens and rabbits, so they are carnivores.

## Eating all sorts!

Some animals eat both plants and other creatures. They are called **omnivores**. Humans are omnivores—we eat a mixture of plant and animal foods.

Do snails such as this one enjoy eating one type of leaf more than another?

## Steps to follow

## Watching birds

For this activity you will need:

* A bird feeding platform raised above the ground
* A hanging **seed** or nut bird feeder
* Crusts or crumbs

**1** Put some crusts and crumbs on the bird platform. Hang a seed or nut bird feeder from a corner or from a hook close to it.

**2** Watch the birds that visit your bird platform. Make notes of which types of bird eat from the platform and which eat from the hanging feeder. You will need to keep very still as you watch—sudden movements will scare the birds away. Look at the ways they manage to eat the food: How do they stand or hang, what shapes are their beaks, are they big birds or small birds?

**3** If you have a bird fact book, try to identify some of the birds you see. What are the main differences you can see between those that eat from the flat feeder and those that eat from the hanging feeder?

**Warning**: Make sure your bird platform is safe from cats and other animals that might harm the birds.

# The right type of food

Different creatures eat different types of food, and most are specially suited to the type of food they eat. Ducks have flat beaks to filter weeds from water, and swallows have short, pointed beaks so that they can catch insects in the air. Hummingbirds can hover in one place while they suck nectar from flowers through long, thin beaks. Many birds of **prey** have sharp **talons** for catching and holding small animals. Squirrels have long, sharp front teeth to help them chew nuts. Foxes have sharp teeth at the sides of their mouths for tearing meat and strong back teeth for crushing bones.

This finch's small, pointed beak is ideal for eating seeds.

## Hunters and hunted

You will have noticed from watching the birds that different types of bird eat different foods in different ways. Many living things have to work hard to get their food, while others have to work hard to avoid being eaten! Animals that are hunted by others are called prey. Animals that hunt others are called **predators**. Some animals hunt and are also hunted, so they are both predator and prey.

This owl glides silently at night so its prey does not hear it coming until it is too late!

## Prey animals

Many prey animals have special **adaptations**, which help them to avoid being caught. Large ears help rabbits and hares sense danger approaching, and strong back legs help them run fast to escape. Being the same color as the surroundings can help prey animals to hide from predators. This is called **camouflage**. Some caterpillars are green, which makes them almost invisible against leaves and stems. Some creatures have markings that make them look dangerous and scare off other creatures that might want to eat them. Others, such as some salamanders, make poison that oozes out of their skin when they are attacked.

## Predators

Many predators also have special adaptations to help them get their food. Sharks have excellent senses of smell and hearing, which help them to locate their prey. Spiders spin webs to trap their prey. Some frogs and lizards have long, sticky tongues that they can shoot out very quickly to catch insects. Some scorpions and snakes can inject poison into their prey to kill it. The long, thin snouts of spiny anteaters are ideal for poking into anthills to search for ants.

Long legs for wading and a long beak for fishing help this heron to catch its food in shallow waters.

## When food is scarce

In winter food can become scarce. Living things have to find ways of coping with this shortage. Some animals, such as brown bears, sleep until food becomes plentiful again. This is called **hibernation**. Others, such as squirrels, store food so that they can eat it when nothing else is available. Some animals, such as many birds, move to areas where there is plenty of food. This is called **migration**.

# Chains and Webs

Living things are linked together by the food that they eat. A simple set of links is called a **food chain**. We can build a food chain:

Green plants, such as grasses, trap energy from the sun to make their food. They are called **producers**. Green plants are the first living things in the food chain.

A **herbivore**, such as a rabbit, eats the grass. It is the first living thing in the food chain to eat anything. It is called the first **consumer**.

A **carnivore**, such as a fox, eats the rabbit. The fox is the second living thing in the food chain to eat anything. It is called the second consumer. Because nothing eats the fox, it is also called the top carnivore.

Plants such as this cereal crop trap the energy from sunlight to make their food.

Food chains are drawn from left to right. Arrows join one living thing to the next. Each arrow means "is eaten by."

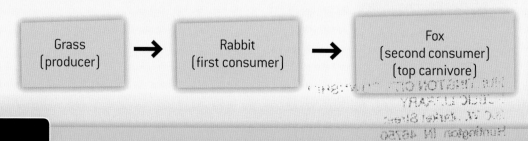

Grass (producer) → Rabbit (first consumer) → Fox (second consumer) (top carnivore)

## Longer chains

Food chains can have more links than this. Look at this food chain:

| Pondweeds | → | Tadpoles | → | Minnows | → | Pike | → | Otter |

The pondweeds trap the energy in sunlight to make food for the plants, so they are the producers. The tadpoles eat the pondweed, so they are the first consumers. Moving along the chain, the minnows are the second consumers, and the pike are the third consumers. The otter is the fourth consumer—and because nothing eats the otter, it is also the top carnivore.

## Predator, prey, or both?

Trying to decide which creatures are **predators** and which are **prey** can be complicated! Here is another food chain:

| Leaves | → | Caterpillars | → | Robins | → | Hawk |

The caterpillars get eaten by the robins, so they are prey.

The hawk eats the robins, so it is a predator.

But what about the robins? They eat the caterpillars, but they then get eaten by the hawk—so the robins are both predators and prey!

This hare eats grass—but it may get eaten by another animal.

# Different habitats, different food chains

Different things live in different **habitats**. Therefore, the food chains in one habitat are different from those in another habitat. Look at these examples. Can you figure out which are the producers in each? Which are the top carnivores? Which are the first and second consumers? Which creatures are predator and which are prey?

A food chain from a forest habitat:

Grass → Grasshopper → Frog → Snake → Hawk

An Arctic food chain:

**Krill** → Shrimp → Arctic cod → Seal → Polar bear

A desert food chain:

Mesquite bush → Ant → Lizard → Snake

A cold mountain habitat food chain:

Water plants → Small fish → Salmon → Brown bear

Brown bears are **omnivores**, but fish are an important part of their diet. They are skilled at catching fish from the river!

# Where do they go?

Have you ever questioned what happens to dead plants and animals? If they simply stayed where they died, a habitat would soon be piled high with dead leaves, branches, flowers, and bodies! Animals get run over on roads, but they do not stay there forever. So, where do they go? The answer is they get eaten! Some plants and creatures live off dead plant and animal material.

These millipedes live off dead plant and animal material.

There are three main types of plants and creatures that live off dead plants and animals:

## Scavengers

**Scavengers** eat meat, but they let other animals do the hard work for them! They live off animals that have died or have been killed by other animals. Vultures, raccoons, crows, spider crabs, and blowflies are all scavengers. Some scavengers hunt and kill for food in addition to scavenging.

## Detritivores

**Detritivores** live off dead and decaying plant and animal remains. Worms, millipedes, cockroaches, and many types of beetle are detritivores.

## Decomposers

**Decomposers** live off dead and decaying plant and animal material, as well as the waste from scavengers and detritivores. Most decomposers, such as bacteria and fungi, are too small for us to see without a microscope. Some fungi, though, are much bigger. They are the plant-like structures that we call mushrooms and toadstools.

## Make a food chain mobile

For this activity you will need:

* Cardboard
* Scissors
* Sticky tape
* Crayons or felt pens
* Thread or string

**1** Choose a habitat and write out a food chain that could be found there. For example, if you chose a woodland habitat, your food chain might be:

Oak leaves → Caterpillars → Robins → Hawk

**2** On a thin piece of cardboard draw, color (on both sides), and cut out a picture about 4 inches (10 cm) tall of your top carnivore. In this food chain it would be a hawk. Then draw, color, and cut out two smaller pictures of its prey. Here it would be two robins. Then draw and cut out four smaller pictures of their prey. Here it would be four caterpillars. Then draw and cut out eight smaller pictures of whatever they eat. Here it would be eight oak leaves.

Use sticky tape to attach two threads to the bottom of the top carnivore. Attach each thread to the top of one of its prey pictures. Repeat until all the creatures and plants are linked together. Attach a strong thread to the top of the top carnivore, and your mobile is ready to be hung up.

## Scavengers, decomposers, and detritivores in food chains

You can link scavengers, decomposers, and detritivores into food chains for different habitats:

In this woodland food chain, the earthworm is a detritivore.

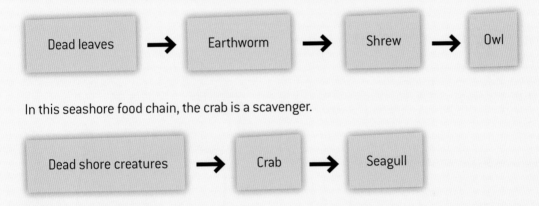

| Dead leaves | → | Earthworm | → | Shrew | → | Owl |

In this seashore food chain, the crab is a scavenger.

| Dead shore creatures | → | Crab | → | Seagull |

## Natural recycling

All these things work together like a natural, never-ending, recycling machine!

The sharp, hooked beaks of these vultures are excellent for tearing meat.

## What is a food web?

Food chains are a simple way of showing feeding links between the plants and animals living in a habitat. It is usually more complicated than this, though. What happens if two different creatures both eat the same sort of plant? Or if two carnivores both hunt the same smaller creatures? You can imagine the way links in chains get tangled up—this is exactly what happens in food chains. Two or more food chains can be linked together to make a **food web**.

## In a woodland

Look at these woodland food chains:

Green plants → Slug → Thrush → Hawk

Green plants → Rabbit → Fox

Green plants → Rabbit → Hawk

**Seeds** → Mouse → Fox

Seeds → Mouse → Owl

Seeds → Finch → Hawk

Can you see how the same living things appear in more than one chain?

This food web shows all the individual food chains and how they are linked together.

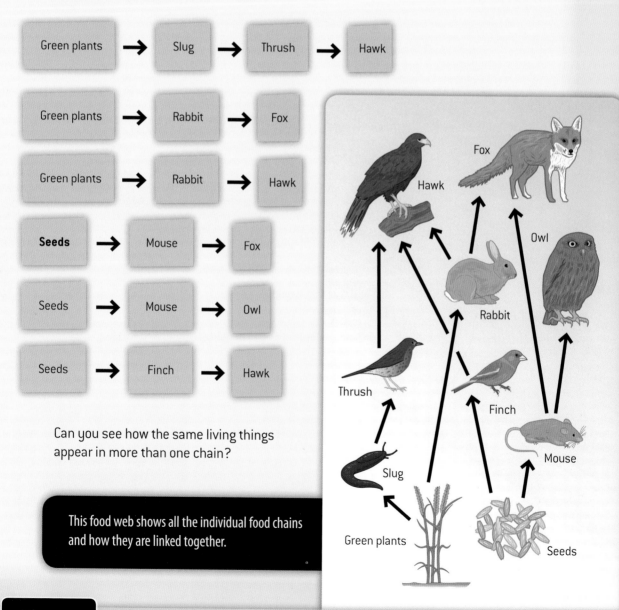

40

## Habitat balance

The living things within a habitat are carefully balanced. Each has the right amount of food to survive. If one type of living thing dies, the whole habitat is affected. Imagine what would happen in the woodland if the green plants died. The rabbit and slug would have nothing to eat, so they would die, too. The thrush would die because there would be no slugs for it to eat. The hawk and fox would need to eat more finches and mice to make up for the lack of rabbits and thrushes—so the hawk, fox, and owl would all be competing for the same foods.

## Competition

There can also be a problem if one type of living thing suddenly increases in number. Imagine the same woodland again if the foxes have more cubs than usual. They will eat more rabbits and mice, so the owl and hawk will be competing for the finches.

A hedgehog is not the only type of creature that thinks a snail is a tasty snack.

# Conclusion

Wildlife is amazing! Wherever you live there will always be something unexpected to see. Gardens, parks, woodlands, deserts, ponds, seashores, forests—there are many different **habitats** to explore. There are millions of different living things on our planet, from microscopic fungi to giant redwood trees, from spiny porcupines to furry chinchillas, from creepy caterpillars to soaring eagles. There are too many to name! Whatever you are interested in, and wherever you live, there is sure to be some sort of wildlife that you can enjoy watching.

It may not seem a big climb to us, but just think how hard this caterpillar must have worked to reach the tip of the leaf!

## Wildlife in your garden

If you have a garden, you can help to attract wildlife to it. Look for plants or packages of **seeds** that say they attract butterflies or other insects. A small garden pond can be home to frogs and other creatures. Seed heads left over after plants have finished flowering will attract seed-eating birds. Bird feeders will attract birds to visit your garden for food. Birdhouses, bat houses, and insect houses will attract these creatures to come and live in the garden.

## Get involved!

The plants and animals that share our planet are important. They are also really interesting. Some are brightly colored, some look strange, and others behave in very odd ways! Why not get to know the wildlife around you? If you start watching wildlife, you will be amazed by what you see!

## Don't get too close!

All living things are important. Many living things are protected by law and must not be moved or picked. Some are poisonous or can harm you in other ways. You may also harm a creature if you get too close. For example, a parent bird may desert its nest and young if it feels threatened by the presence of a human. It is usually best to look and watch, but not to touch.

Male green anoles puff out their throats to attract females!

# Glossary

**adaptation** something special about a living thing that helps it to live in its habitat. An adaptation of a cactus is that it can store water so it can survive in a very dry habitat.

**algae** type of plant that lives in water or damp places. Seaweeds are all algae.

**amphibian** creature that has smooth, wet skin, breathes with gills and often lungs, and lays its eggs in water. A frog is an amphibian.

**antennae** thin, wavy structures on the heads of some invertebrates. Antennae help invertebrates to sense the world around them.

**aphid** type of tiny insect that feeds on plants. Greenfly and whitefly are aphids.

**camouflage** color or patterns on a creature that blend in with its surroundings. An Arctic hare has white fur to camouflage it among the snow and ice.

**carnivore** animal that eats other animals. Eagles and wolves are both carnivores.

**characteristic** special quality about something that makes it different from another thing. Two characteristics of a crocodile are sharp teeth and dry, scaly skin.

**conifer** tree that has needle-like leaves and makes cones. Most Christmas trees are conifers.

**consumer** anything that eats something else. You are a consumer when you eat a cheese sandwich or a bar of chocolate!

**decomposer** living thing that breaks down dead material and releases nutrients. Mushrooms and toadstools are decomposers.

**detritivore** creature that eats dead and decaying plant and animal material. Millipedes and cockroaches are detritivores.

**fern** type of plant that has fronds for leaves and makes spores

**fin** structure on the back and underside of a fish that helps it to swim. They may not look it, but fins can be very strong.

**flowering plant** plant that has flowers and makes seeds. Sunflowers and thistles are both flowering plants.

**food chain** way that living things are linked by their food. This is an example of a simple food chain: pondweed is eaten by tadpoles, which are eaten by newts.

**food web** way that several food chains are joined together. Food webs show feeding links in a habitat.

**frond** branching leaf of a fern plant. The branches of a frond are biggest near the plant and get smaller and smaller toward the tip.

**gill** part of fish and amphibians that enables them to breathe in water. People have lungs instead of gills, so we cannot breathe in water.

**habitat** place where a plant or creature lives. A duck's habitat is a pond or lake, and an earthworm's habitat is soil.

**herbivore** creature that only eats plants. Deer and rabbits are both herbivores.

**hibernation** sleeping through the winter. Brown bears hibernate as winter approaches and wake up again when the warm spring comes.

**invertebrate** creature without a backbone. Butterflies, jellyfish, and beetles are all invertebrates.

**krill** tiny invertebrates that live in the sea. Larger sea creatures such as shrimps eat krill.

**magnifying glass**  curved piece of glass that makes things look bigger than they really are. Using a magnifying glass helps you to see things you cannot see with your eyes alone.

**mammal**  creature with hair or fur whose babies develop inside the mother and drink the mother's milk after birth. Humans, elephants, and moles are all mammals.

**migration**  moving to a different place for a while and then coming back again. Many birds migrate to a warmer place during the winter and then come back in the spring.

**moss**  simple plants that have leaves but no true roots. You can see mosses growing on old stones and in damp, shady places.

**nocturnal**  name given to creatures that are active mainly at night. Badgers and owls are nocturnal.

**omnivore**  animal that eats both meat and plants. Mostly humans are omnivores.

**predator**  animal that hunts and kills other animals for food. Crocodiles and coyotes are both predators.

**prey**  animal that is hunted by other animals and eaten. Tadpoles, mice, and sparrows are all prey.

**producer**  anything that makes its own food. All green plants are producers—they produce their own food using energy from sunlight.

**reptile**  animal that has dry scales, breathes with lungs, lives in water or on land, and lays soft-shelled eggs on land. Turtles and snakes are both reptiles.

**scale**  small piece that fits together with others to make the outer covering of fish and reptiles. Mammals have fur and birds have feathers, but fish and reptiles have scales.

**scavenger**  animal that does not hunt but does eat dead animals. Vultures and spider crabs are both scavengers.

**seed**  part of a flowering plant that will grow into a new plant. Apple pips are the seeds of an apple tree.

**spore**  part of a fern that will grow into a new plant. You can see spores as brown spots on the back of the fern fronds.

**talon**  strong, sharp claw of a bird of prey. Talons are good for catching small animals or birds.

**tide**  regular movement of the sea back and forth over the seashore. The times of the tides change every day.

**vertebrate**  creature that has a backbone. Snakes, whales, and parrots are all vertebrates.

# Find Out More

## Books

Amato, Carol. *Backyard Pets: Activities for Exploring Wildlife Close to Home*. New York: John Wiley & Sons, 2002.

Hodgkins, Fran. *Animals Among Us: Living with Suburban Wildlife*. North Haven, Conn.: Linnet, 2000.

Jackson, Tom, and Michael Chinery. *The Illustrated Encyclopedia of Animals in America*. Lanham, Md.: Lorenz, 2006.

Kerrod, Robin, and John Stidworthy. *Facts on File: Facts on File Wildlife Atlas*. New York: Facts on File, 2002.

Stetson, Emily. *Kids' Easy-to-Create Wildlife Habitats*. Nashville, Tenn.: Williamson, 2004.

Taylor, Barbara. *Urban Wildlife Habitats*. Milwaukee: Gareth Stevens, 2006.

Young, Caroline, and Kate Needham. *Great Wildlife Search*. Tulsa, Okla.: Usborne/EDC, 2004.

# Websites

Kidsplanet

**www.kidsplanet.org/factsheets/map.html**

Electronic fact sheets on over 50 species of animal.

National Geographic

**www.nationalgeographic.com**

Huge site giving lots of information about animals. There is a special section for kids where there are videos, games, and activities.

Kids Go Wild Conservation Society

**www.kidsgowild.com**

Information on wild animals and conservation. Puzzles and activities are also available.

Wildlife Trust

**www.wildlifetrust.org**

Information about the different projects that aim to preserve wildlife.

# Organizations

**National Audubon Society**

700 Broadway, New York, New York 10003
www.audubon.org

**National Wildlife Federation**

11100 Wildlife Center Drive, Reston, Virginia 20190
www.nwf.org

**World Wildlife Fund**

1250 Twenty-Fourth Street, N.W., P.O. Box 97180, Washington, D.C. 20090-7180
www.worldwildlife.org

# Index